THE HURT OF A HEALED WOMAN:

Hidden Gems

Dr. Constance Hope Seals, D.C.

Cover designed by Nskvsky

Printed in the United States of America
First Printing: August 2022
The Scribe Tribe Publishing Group

THE SCRIBE TRIBE
PUBLISHING GROUP

ISBN-978-1-958436-05-9 (ebook)

ISBN – 978-1-958436-04-2 (print)

Disclaimer:

This is my story! The good, the bad and the unfiltered ugly. This book is not intended to bash anyone just simply to speak my truth and tell my experiences. I hope my story will help other women and men to be bold, courageous and strong within themselves. Know that your circumstances

DO NOT define you and never let anyone ever tell you differently!

Contents

MOTHER

Mother, if you are reading this, what I am about to say is not meant to hurt you; just listen. Where do I start? So many times I questioned you. Never out loud, but in my mind. Why did you never protect us? Why did you never give us those motherly hugs and why did you never speak up? But on that same Sunday as my father, I saw you too. I finally understood you. You had never really told your daughters anything about you, so we did not know you personally. You did not speak much; you were always kind of distant. You kept your house clean, and made sure your man, our father, was taken care of hand and foot, but nothing more.

On that Sunday, I learned that you traveled a lot growing up. I learned how much you loved your brothers and your twin. You told me your dreams, goals and all that you wanted to accomplish. But you also told me the things you have been through. All this, I could not see at first, well ever before. I had no clue.

You took all that you went through and bottled it up. Never speaking of those ill acts or wrongdoings done to you ever again. You were never weak. You just felt there was no time to deal with those things, and if you did, it would hurt too much to do so.

I see you, mother. Know that I see you.

I see the woman that is now starting to stick up for herself, stand her ground, finding her voice. You are awakening. Sound familiar? I came from you, so if I can do it, you can too. You are stronger than you think.

Your story is just beginning so that is all for now. I will let you tell your own!

YOU START
HOW YOU WANT
TO FINISH

It has always been said, "You start how you want to finish." But, if the way I came into this world was ANY consolation of what my life would be like, oh boy, folks! Hold on to your seats because this is going to escalate quickly. Three weeks prior to me being born, my father was in a coma. They did not expect him to live and had made their medical decision about his condition. The medical team gave my mother two options. One, to pull the plug. Or two, they would leave him on life support, but they believed he would not have a good quality of life if he survived. They had determined he would likely be a vegetable, wheelchair bound, unable to ever write, speak or walk again. During this tragic time, my mother was nearing her due date for me to be born. With my mother and father three hours apart, in two different hospitals, something miraculous happened.

My mom gave birth to me on Sunday, February 23, 1992. But shockingly, my dad woke up from his coma at the exact same time I was born. Unknown to my mother at the time, she named me Constance Hope because she was constantly hoping and praying my father would wake from his coma. And he did. He is alive and well, still today. Thirty years later, he is still walking, talking and preaching. He became a minister after his accident. He has no visible traces of ever being in a coma other than his scars and of course some residual brain trauma. It is interesting when I hear my father talk about his near-death experience and what happened when he woke up.

He said the first thing he saw when he came out of the coma was baby shoes.

That alone is amazing since they were three hours away from each other. So, on my birthday every year, my family would say, "Happy Birthday, Constance," with an added tradition of then turning to my dad saying, "And happy re-birth day to you, dad."

That being said you might suspect there have been some pretty wild and amazing things I have experienced in my life.

FATHER

You never really know how many issues or skeletons you have until you start unpacking yourself and looking deeper within. As a woman, most know that, even if it is unintentionally, we tend to choose guys like our father. And sometimes, without realizing it, we pick a "father figure" substitute in a guy. I believe it works the same for males when choosing a mate. They gravitate to a woman like their mom. This can be a good thing or a bad thing, depending on your upbringing.

If I am transparent, my father was not the best "father figure." In some degree of defense, you tend to do things that were done to you or that you feel is the "right way to parent." However, some things are inexcusable.

My home was not filled with love and laughter nor meaningful, deep father-daughter talks or mother-daughter talks either, for that matter. So many people take those things for granted. Oh, how I always longed for those conversations, those moments and those good memories. Sadly, looking back on my childhood, I don't have many. No family vacations, road trips or random things to cling to.

The only things that stuck were the trauma. The methods used for "discipline" were not okay in any shape, form or fashion. Now that I am older, it is amazing to realize that as much as I tried to stay away from the craziness of the house, I was still affected in more ways than I thought.

When I was a teenager, I would try to find ways to escape my reality which meant staying away from the house during the day for as long as possible to avoid going home and only going home to sleep.

If you were to ask my sisters their version of my experience in the house, they would probably say the opposite. They always saw me as the "golden child," the one who "did no wrong," and they were right to an extent. But why was I so golden is the question no one ever seemed to ask.

I would bury myself in my studies and extracurricular activities. I was what most would call very well-rounded. During high school, I got good grades. I was in choir, varsity track, and captain of the step team. I was also an executive chef at *The Savvy's Bistro,* a restaurant located within a culinary arts academy that my school partnered with.

But why so golden?

Well, a few reasons.

There was so much going on at the house. My two sisters were always getting into some sort of trouble which took all of my parents' attention and focus. So, one reason was to just get away and stay out as long as I could to not have to go home to the chaos. The other reason was because I desperately wanted my parent's attention, support and love. Three simple things that I felt I never really got. I remember things so vividly.

It was my junior year of high school. I was pretty good at track, to say the least. To be on varsity as a junior was tough to accomplish. There was one track meet I remember in particular. My position on the track team was in the 4 by 1-first leg. We ran that meet and I received a first-place metal. I was so proud of myself. As I looked around to see where my parents were, I quickly noticed that they were nowhere to be found.

I saw my sisters far away standing by the gated fence. I shuffled over to them after I won and said, "Where's mom and dad?" My older sister responded, "They told me to come pick you up after you were done. But you did a good job on your race, little sister." I gave her a quick side smile because I did not want her to know I was upset. I turned and walked to the bleachers to grab my things and tears came to my eyes. Two weeks later I decided to quit track. I figured why put in all the effort to try to make them proud and get their attention if being the best still did not cause them to even look in my direction, notice or come to support.

After that, I found my next escape, which was working long hours as a hostess at Razoo's Cajun Restaurant in Arlington, Texas. However, that was not my first time working. I had my first job at 15 years old, working with my sisters at the Dallas Fort Worth Airport. Then I worked at Whataburger, Six Flags, Big League Dreams Baseball field, Razoo's and then back to the airport the summer of my senior year of high school before heading off to college.

However, part of the curse of working so young is that if I didn't do it, I felt it would not get done. That in turn had me take on much more than I should have and a lot of people depended on me and still do. That is such a large and heavy load to carry.

I created my own mobile real estate closing company in 2020. After creating my company, it jump started my self-discovery journey. It made me ask, "Wow, what else did I not know about myself?" I never would have thought in a million years that I would or could be a successful CEO. I started digging deeper and looking inwardly at myself. What I found was actually quite shocking.

The not so funny thing of it all was I tried to stay away from the chaos of my house and thought if I stayed away then I would not be affected by the things that occurred within it. I was the only one, being the youngest of three sisters, to go to college. I had a good relationship with my significant other and I felt I was doing okay for myself. I had made it out of that house without a scratch or so I thought.

BOY, WAS I WRONG!

I started down that path of self-discovery which unveiled a lot of things about me I didn't know existed. My self-discovery journey came at a very random, unexpected time. It began after I decided to quit my job and start my own company. After just a few short months, my company was doing amazing! In six months of starting that company, I had managed to partner with some heavy hitters in the industry, which took me by surprise. The first time I fully bet on myself, I was rewarded greatly. However, that did get me thinking. What else can Constance do? There obviously is more to Constance, but what? And so, it began. The start of my discovery and the quest to find me.

Things started to surface when I went off to college. But it was typical me. I saw the problem, worked on it myself and finally got to a resolution. At that point, I thought I had gotten my skeletons under control. Therefore, I truly thought the worst was behind me. I would later find that to be untrue. We will get into the backstory of what I unveiled about myself a little later on.

Father: The Insider

I thought I finally got to the root of the problem. As stated previously, my sisters tended to get wrapped up in many things, some of which trickled into their adult lives. Unfortunately, one of my sisters got into an altercation with an abusive boyfriend that landed her in prison. She was sentenced to three years, not to be released until April 2022. As expected, discussions about my sister's release from prison caused quite the conversations amongst our family.

I thought everybody would genuinely be on board with helping my sister to do well. I am not sure why I felt anything had changed, maybe it was because we were all adults now. However, we were never really the family unit type growing up. We all started to try to piece together what roles we would play when she got out.

I had a conversation with my parents where I stated my position on my sister's release. I assured them that I would 100 percent, without a shadow of a doubt help her in any way I could. To my surprise, my father was not so enthusiastic. He was not so eager to help. I was furious and I demanded to know why. And then it happened. We finally got to the root of the problem. As my father started to tell me how he had always tried for his family, even after a serious brain injury, we began to dig deeper and I realized something.

Although once again inexcusable, I realized my dad was suffering from a broken heart. He told me stories of my sister when she was younger. How she would put on his suit coats, run around the house and how she never left his side. She was so upset when I was born because she always wanted to be daddy's baby girl and the youngest. He lastly mentioned, "And now that daughter is gone. She changed. She's not like that anymore and hasn't been for as long as I can remember."

There it was! Finally, I saw that stubborn man's heart and his hurt. This was one of the rare times in my whole 29 years of life. I think at the moment it was the first time I really saw my father.

SISTER, SISTER

Growing up, my sisters and I were all we really had. Growing up in the projects, we knew we always had to watch each other's back outside of the house. But inside it was ALWAYS a different story. I was the youngest of the three of us. My two older sisters were like Cain and Abel, the hateful brothers from the Bible. Constantly fighting each other so much I really thought they were going to take each other out. Those who know them understand it was an equal and mutual fighting situation, in and out of the house. Nevertheless, no one could mess with one of us outside those walls.

It was the same when it came to making sure each other was making it. My oldest sister was basically like our mother. My dad worked long hours at work and so did my mom, then they would do things together on the weekends. So, it was basically just us. My oldest sister and I never saw eye to eye. I always thought she was way too bossy and could not know much more than me since we were only two and half years apart. But she was how I kept my head above water. The three of us were always resourceful. Although, my oldest sister could not drive worth a damn!

There was this time when we all got jobs at the airport. My oldest sister had just recently gotten her driver's license and I did not feel particularly comfortable about her driving skills to say the least. But, of course, she was assigned to drive us to work. I remember one day she drove us to work, I was gazing out the window when we passed a stop sign that I read backwards.

That's when I realized she was driving down a one-way street. As I started to scream, I signaled my sister with, "HEY, I DON'T THINK THIS IS RIGHT! I THINK YOU'RE GOING THE WRONG," A car drove right up to us, head on. Thank God for the great skills of the other driver because I am quite sure my oldest sister pooped herself that day! The other driver had missed us by just a few feet from a head-on collision accident.

After gathering what was left of her soul, my sister ducked down behind the wheel of the car and backed slowly to the main road and then drove off. Finally, we started rolling again on our way to work. A little way down the street, we all looked at each other and burst out hysterically in laughter. Then, it got pitch quiet and remained quiet for the rest of the way there. We were 17, 16 and 15 years old.

About a month prior, my two older sisters told me they wanted to check out a place that was hiring for positions at the airport. They said they would pick me up after school so they could go apply. Getting a job at the airport meant they would be gone most of the day. I knew I would be at the house alone if I did not act fast.

Y'all before I knew it, I had mustered up the courage to talk to the lady who had just hired them. I pleaded with her that I could do the same work they were doing! She looked at me puzzled but she saw I was very serious.

She reluctantly said "Well okay, but your sisters would have to sign a release form saying they will watch you while you are at work because you're under age."

Done! They signed it and I had my very first official job!

I felt so cool! I could finally be independent and make a ton of money because we also got tips. But the best part was not having to ask my parents for anything.

Although it was taxing on the body, pushing wheelchairs with people of all sizes up and down the jet bridge, I loved that job! Well at least the first time anyway. I worked at the airport again the summer of my senior year. It was cool, but it was better when I was first hired at age 15. Things were much more relaxed. I mean, how many 15-year-old teenagers are walking around with a wad of cash and giving people lunch money? However, what I did not realize was that I was starting an unhealthy trend of "do it yourself" that would later be a blessing and a curse.

A blessing because I started so young that it taught me how to become an independent woman. How to get out there and grind for what I needed, how to bounce back and how to budget my money. The curse was that I *had* to know these traits at such a young age. It was like survival mode. I knew that if I did not do these things for myself, I would go without. From the age of fifteen all the way through my senior year of high school, I held a job. I bought my own everything! Own clothes, own shoes, own school supplies, even down to my own under clothes. That which was instilled in me at such a young age was NOT a lesson I wanted to learn so soon.

Working so much and being overly involved in extracurricular activities really robbed me of childhood and normal teenage things. While most were going out to parties, sleepovers and other teenage festivities, I was working to make sure I had what I needed.

Now that I am older, one thing that has helped me regain some of my childhood is traveling! I love to travel and I do it as frequently as I can. It is the only time I can actually let go of my own responsibilities, just live life and have fun.

NO MORE US

I t's funny when you get out of high school most people cannot wait to go to college because they finally feel like they can become an adult and make their own decisions. True, in college you do have more freedom and your success is predicated specifically on your choices. However, college also gives you a safe haven before real life hits you. You are given room and board, meal plans, refund checks and student jobs are available so everything is convenient and on hand.

You know what sounds good in theory? Starting from the bottom with someone. Staying together through the struggles. While I think that does show your heart in those situations, it is only to a certain extent. For my ex and I that theory was put to the test.

My ex-husband and I met when we were very young. I was 18, he was 19. We crossed paths my freshman year of undergrad when he was a sophomore. Same major and minor at Prairie View A&M University. Like most relationships, things were going well at first because we were still in the college bubble. No real-life things had happened to us yet. We were really close and people admired our relationship. However, we still struggled like the typical college students. My ex and I were broke!

Once during my junior year, we went to a Texas A&M game with some friends. We only had a few dollars to put together. We were hungry, but too embarrassed to say anything to our friends. We all went to McDonald's. My ex and I knew the situation; we only had enough to get one McDouble, a small fry and a cup of water. We split that McDouble in half so we could eat. No one knew we did that until years later. But for us, that seemed to be only the beginning to our struggles.

THE FINAL
TURNING POINT

I think the final turning point for me was in 2018. It's interesting because that was the year I got married and it was almost immediately after doing so. My ex had decided to join a fraternity. During that time, he was still a student in pharmacy school and I was working as an associate doctor at a new practice. We were preparing for our wedding which was just a few months out. We had recently moved from a small apartment into a house.

Things started to become very expensive and tight for us. Well, like joining any fraternity or sorority, it can be very time consuming. That is exactly what happened in his situation. He would go to school during the day and do things with the fraternity at night. This cut our financial supply way down. He didn't have time to work, go to school and do fraternity related events. This brought us to one paycheck—mine. So, planning for a wedding, which was about 2-3 months away, and starting a new job was a juggling act. I was still on my 90-day probation period at my new job, so I was not even getting my full pay yet.

There were so many times he could not be there because he had no time. So, it was all up to me. Well, the wedding day finally came and, somehow, we managed to pay it off. Our wedding was on a weekend and we literally only got to spend Sunday, the day of the wedding, together. The very next morning he had to go right back into doing things with his fraternity.

That was an odd feeling for me. I did a lot of pondering that week while I was home alone in that empty house. *Is this what marriage is? Did I put unrealistic expectations on what marriage is like?*

With my ex and I meeting in college, after a few years of dating, we moved in together. We split bills, groceries and other things. Living together was not new for us, so after the wedding it seemed like it was just another day and I felt very uneasy about the situation. Nothing had changed. We did not even have the time to do the honeymoon stage of marriage, nor have an actual honeymoon for that matter.

About a month after our nuptials, shit hit the fan! Still not having that time with my new husband was eating at me. We were still spending no time together and then I lost my job. My boss had a very big ego. She would tell patients, "If you like Dr. Constance's adjustment better than mine, don't tell me." As if it was a competition. This was not the first time something like this had happened to me while working in someone else's practice. So, I was leery about what was to come next when I first accepted the job. Sure enough, the head doctor fired me. However, she had intentionally left the office beforehand and made the office manager do the dirty deed. The office manager and I were very close, so this put her in a very awkward position. She was almost in tears as she told me the news. I later found out that the office manager quit shortly after she had to deliver my news, because she reached out to apologize.

I was without a job and that was our only source of income. I am sure you can imagine what came next. Everything came crashing down. My ex happened to be home when I got home from the office. I do believe that was God because I snapped. I mean, I literally snapped. I had a mental breakdown where I was screaming and hollering at the top of my lungs. I threw a fit to the point he had to grab and restrain me from doing more. I was crying uncontrollably and shaking. About an hour later, he got a call from his fraternity that they needed to see him. So, he left. I stayed where I was and cried face down on the floor like a baby. How did I get myself in such a mess and the real question was, "Had I just married my father?"

It started to feel all too familiar. My father was so consumed with matters of the church that his house was metaphorically burning down with his daughters inside. But the church business was his priority. The pattern seemed to continue. My husband left me at the time I needed him the most, for fraternity business.

About a month later, I got a firm knock at the door. I was on the phone with my best friend at the time. It was a police officer coming to serve us eviction papers.

Did I resent that fraternity? I am not going to lie. Yes, because I felt as though my ex put them above his schooling, job, wife/marriage and home life. But when I asked him, "Do you regret it?" The answer I received was, "No." Do not get me wrong, I met some amazing people during that time and made some good memories. However, the things that came with him joining the organization was what I resented the most.

One major takeaway from my divorce was you have to be an individual first to establish a healthy relationship with someone else. As stated previously, my ex and I got together so young at 18 and 19 years old. We did not know what we were doing. We were just trying to make it work. However, we were always so attached at the hip; I was anywhere he was and vice versa.

Looking back, I know now we formed an unhealthy codependency. We were not individuals. Want to measure this in your own life? If you are in a relationship, if the other individual were to leave would you be okay? Could you take care of yourself financially, mentally and physically? Could you stand on your own if need be? If your answer is "yes," congratulations you could be an asset to a relationship, not a liability. If your answer is "no," you may also, unknowingly, be experiencing codependency in your relationship.

If a person has to depend on another for their own happiness and finances, among other things, then it is time for that person to do some reflecting. When you have to depend on another individual for these things, you are at their mercy. If that individual were to ever take those away, it would destroy the other person. And that is a dangerous position to be in.

However, when two INDIVIDUALS come together to form a relationship, you gain a partner. Someone who you can grow with, support you, love you and do things alongside you instead of one person taking on the entire load. That is a healthy relationship. Some will even call that a "power couple" because you both are a team. You are great on your own, but looking to team up and join forces.

See I believe a lot of people are marrying wrong. Many people fall in love first and think about the facts of marriage later. But in reality, those facts matter upfront. As stated before, it is important to be an individual. When two strong individuals collide, you are really starting from two strong foundations so you are able to build on top of that.

Think of it like a house. Each side of the house is essential to the other. Without all four sides or walls, the house would fall. So why would you get into a relationship with the walls missing. You would then not only have to uphold your own walls, with one hand to keep it from falling, you would also have to single-handedly build the other walls too.

So many are in an identity crisis and do not even know it. They did not know themselves truly, so when entering a relationship or an organization they lose themselves even further or completely. Can you genuinely say you know who you are outside of a relationship, family life, kids or an organization you may be in? Who are you? Because those things are attributes, but those things certainly do not define you. So, I ask again, outside of these things, WHO ARE YOU?

Everyone knows their name but how well do you know your SELF? If you cannot tell me who you are, you will always get lost in translation. If you do not know yourself, how can you stand on your beliefs? That means those beliefs are not your own. You must believe in yourself first and know yourself well before you bring another individual in or you are sure to lose the little you did know about yourself.

THE GHOST OF APRIL'S PAST

What you are about to read might be disturbing, but please read it in its entirety.

It came from a very dark place I was at in my life. I thought about not including this in the book because it was so personal to me. Yet, I added it because someone out there needs to hear and see this to know you can make it out alive. This is a personal letter I wrote to myself in my journal on April 11, 2021.

4/11/2021-The RE- Discovery of Me

Who is Constance??
What does she want?
Is she someone she can look in the mirror each day?
Can you trust her?
Do you love her?
Who TF is Constance?
Did she lose who Constance is?

LORD, I NEED YOUR HELP

How do I re-fix my mental?
I don't actually know what I want but not sure what I'm searching for???

Why am I so unhappy?
My life isn't bad.
Why do I feel so alone when I am not?
Why do I feel no one cares, when they do??
Why is my brain so foggy?
Why do I feel myself slipping?
Someone help, why do I feel like there isn't anyone I can call when I've done so much for other people?

Why don't people think I need love?
Why am I now seeking attention???? Seeking approval of others.
Is it because I never got support at home and now it's rearing its ugly head and haunting me present day? YES
But Why now? I've been fine until NOW.

What changed???
Are my feelings true and accurate or is it all in my head?
This causes me to go back into my shell
This makes me push people away...

I need help but no one understands...
No one cares...
My heart hurts! I am conflicted and torn
Do I follow my heart or do I follow my messed-up mind?

Can she be a wife? Can she be a mother? Does she still want those things?
YES...I think
Is she still kind and gentle?
Did she lose her innocence?

Why does she feel SOOO alone?
Was there a trigger?
Is it due to past trauma from home or issues now???
OR BOTH? But WHY NOW? WHY RESURFACE NOW??

Is this discovery or pain?
What pain have you not healed from BUT WHY NOW??

Later, I spoke to some friends and family about how I was feeling. I did not go into much detail; I just told them I was considering getting a divorce. The words and advice I received did not help, it actually made things worse.

Journal continues...

4/13/2021
So, I'm a selfish bitch because I want better for myself??
Being committed and faithful for almost 11 years and being the rock!
I need someone else to be the rock for me for a change. I deserve that!!...

So, am I selfish for that shit???
Am I looking at this shit all wrong? AM I THE SELFISH ONE???

This would have been my suicide note. I did not realize it at the time, but shortly after this I contemplated suicide many times. Honestly, re-reading this note is very tough and it scares me. I did not know how lost I was, until looking back on it now.

It is so important to check on your friends and loved ones because you never know what they are actually going through. Just because it looks pretty as a picture, it is important that you understand the person behind it. A lot of people walk around everyday wearing their smiles like a mask. Hiding away their hurt and pain, putting on a brave face for others when they are crumbling.

Never take life or your loved ones for granted. You never know when it could be the last time you speak to them.

We all need to be more vocal about mental health and the issues we go through. Because your stories and testimonies could save someone else's life. Do not be selfish and keep that to yourself to try to keep up your status or to save face. When we speak out about these things, we can stop a lot of unnecessary deaths. Most of the time, the person experiencing it is not thinking clearly in the first place. They just need to hear a voice of reason.

And for those going through this, know that you ultimately determine your future outcome. You can change anything or situation you are in, if you choose to live another day. There should always be at least one person you can call if you ever feel like you cannot take it anymore. If you do not have that person, I encourage you to go out and find that one.

If you are currently in a crisis and you do not have anyone, please call for help.

I was in a situation where I did not have anyone to call and I did not call a prevention hotline. I just talked myself through it. PLEASE do not do that. Get the help you need to get you through this momentary spot in your life that is making you think your life is not worth living. Because it is literally just that, a moment. This too shall pass. (Please go read 2 Corinthians 4:17-18.)

{National Suicide Prevention Lifeline - 1-800-273-8255}

I think more people need to know ways to combat depression. It starts with your thoughts and not letting those negative thoughts consume you. That's literally what depression is, an overwhelming amount of negative thoughts at one time.

Speak something POSITIVE about yourself every time a negative thought pops into your head. It begins here:

Philippians 4:6-9: Don't worry about anything, but pray and ask God for everything you need, always giving thanks for what you have. And because you belong to Christ Jesus, God's peace will stand guard over all your thoughts and feelings. His peace can do this far better than our human minds. Brothers and sisters, continue to think about what is good and worthy of praise. Think about what is true, honorable, right and pure and beautiful and respected. And do what you learned and received from me- what I told you and what you saw me do. And the God who gives peace will be with you.

LOVE AND ITS UNREALISTIC ASS EXPECTATIONS

They say love conquers all and I believe that to a certain extent. However, what I do know is that love also makes you stupid as hell. When you love someone, you do things you wouldn't normally do. Things that otherwise would go against your own intuition. Love will make you have so much faith and trust in a person that they would never do anything to hurt you or jeopardize what you both have. Rather that is love for a parent, family member, significant other or friend, love still is hotwired the same way for all of them. Well, at least it was for me. Yes, there are levels to love, but it's all love nevertheless.

Letting your guard down for someone can be extremely scary. For me it was almost panic attack scary. After all I have been through, when someone gets close to me, I always side eye and question their motives. Some might call it a trust issue; I think it is just me being more cautious and guarded about who I am letting in. I believe that's how most humans do with anyone new in their life. However, for me, I just never had that mindset. Some would say I was being naïve, and looking back on it they were probably right. I've always chalked it up to me being "too nice," but I'll put it like this. When someone new came around and we had good conversation or interaction with no bad energy, I would say, "Okay, I like this person. They are okay in my book. "But then I had a major period of self-discovery that drastically made me change and look at things differently in my life.

What I realized is that I would give them a 100% score to start off with. Wrong answer! After talking to a friend, she told me, "Constance, you have to start people at ground zero. Then add and remove points as they show and prove themselves." It made complete sense! It honestly made me take a deeper look at ALL of my relationships with people in general. I noticed why I got so angry at people when they did something "wrong" or made a mistake. It was because of my subconscious scale. Putting people at a 100 instantly was ultimately a setup for me to get disappointed with people in my life over and over again.

People are only human and are going to make mistakes, so giving them a perfect score puts unrealistic expectations on literally everyone. If you are at 100, even in school, the only thing you can do is decrease unless you keep getting all 100s. That is pretty much impossible because nobody is perfect. I had subconsciously put people on a petal that they did not ask to be on. I set myself up to be disappointed again and again all throughout my life, which in return caused me a lot of hurt and pain.

Now, I am not sure why my mind instantly did that, but taking a new approach to people was so different to me. It made a lot more sense to not expect anything from anyone, to let them build and live up to my standard, brick by brick, especially if I did not know them well enough to begin with.

Well, I found I was an equal opportunist. I did the same thing with the ones I loved. I held them to such a standard that anything that went wrong or any mistake they made, took them down a notch in my book. Do not get me wrong, those who you love should be held to some sort of standard because they are past the initial relationship building stages.

If I could give a word of advice, never stay with someone, whether romantic or friendship, who made a mistake that you know in your heart and mind is a deal breaker for you. If you do, you will end up either holding on to the person too tight to the point of suffocation, or unknowingly punishing them everyday for it. It is okay to try to work through situations. I am not suggesting that you drop your partner if an issue arises or if you have a disagreement. However, if you know that was an unforgivable mistake, as hard and painful as it is, you may have to walk away. Because you both will be miserable. One is being watched constantly in fear of that person possibly doing it again.

Personally, I feel that is an unhealthy way to live. When joy leaves the relationship, you are just two bodies coexisting together because you both are too afraid to be alone or to leave. One thing I have learned is that people are like water balloons. If you hold them too tight, they will either a) burst/explode on you or b) try to wiggle out of your hands to get set free.

Secondly, sometimes we just flat out love the wrong people. What sucks the most is that you literally cannot decide or determine who you love; it just kind of happens. No warnings, no heads up. It just overtakes you.

Have you ever experienced the difference between a heartbreak and a heartache? How would you know if you had experienced a heartbreak versus a heartache, you may ask? Well, if you are asking that question, thank your lucky stars because that means you most certainly have NOT experienced a heartache!

A heartache is a different kind of hurt. It cuts deep and it takes a little piece of your heart with it as a souvenir. Honestly, I feel that piece of your heart just does not heal. That scar is permanent. They say time heals all, but something people do not mention is that it may leave a pretty nasty scar. Don't get me wrong, a heartbreak is nothing to play with either. However, I do feel a person can recover decently from a break but not an ache! Man, pull the knife out slowly.

I have always heard the phrase, "Be careful who you love," but I think it should say, "Be careful who you trust and let in to begin with." Do not overlook those red flags and not hold that other person accountable for their actions. They will only do as much as you allow.

Now, not everything about love is bad. I have seen many successful love stories, couples and marriages. And true love is still out there today, despite what is displayed on social media. So, if you find it, cherish it! Some may never have the privilege of experiencing what true, pure love really feels like.

A MONK OF NO EMOTION: INTO THE SHADOWS

The first skeleton that surfaced during college was anger. There was so much that went on in that house, I became what I like to call, "A Monk of No Emotion." I was so used to keeping everything in, not speaking my peace and internalizing it. When I did start to find my voice in college, it might have come out a little rough. You know the phrase, "hurt people, hurt people?" Well, you can say I took that a bit literally. Once I started talking, I did not stop. I did not have a filter. Especially when it came to things that upset me. I was very touchy. Most things that people might have just let roll off their backs, set me off like a firecracker. I would get so angry even if someone was just making a joke.

Needless to say, I had anger issues...bad! Due to me holding things in, once I did start expressing myself and speaking on things that upset me, there was no off switch. I would fly off the handle and I almost got in four fights my freshman year of college. One was with a roommate. That was probably the worst. My roommate and I had to have a meeting with our dorm head. I had to switch rooms with someone down the hall. Yeah, that was fun.

There were a few other run-ins with various students, one which resulted in me yelling outside of a dorm building for that person to come outside. Plus a few others that I am just not going to mention, but I think you get the point. I was a mess! I was reckless. I was even given the nickname, "Killa C." This all came from not knowing how to deal and process my emotions properly. What made me switch, you might ask?

Well, I sat down one day after just missing the boat on getting expelled from school, and I took a hard look at the situation. I was the first of my immediate family to go off to college. I had made it out for all three of us, my two sisters and I. I could not go back to the life I had; college was my only real way out. Therefore, I made the decision. I had to control my rage and learn to not get so angry to the point of wanting to fight. I had to do better. I made a conscious effort moving forward to breathe, think before I spoke, take a step back and analyze the situation before acting. After putting this into practice, I finally got the hang of it! Of course, I still had my moments but wow, what a difference!

Welp, that was just the first skeleton. There were plenty more from where that came from. This became the first of many I didn't even know existed. When I really started taking a deeper look at Constance, I found anger was not the only thing being suppressed. My journey unveiled that I had daddy issues, abandonment issues, low self-esteem and surprisingly, low self-confidence.

The low self-confidence one definitely was a surprise to me; it kind of snuck up on me. I had always been so confident in leadership roles and in my abilities, but apparently there was an area where I lacked inner beauty.

Flashbacking to a week or so prior to the divorce, it was a random night in May of 2021. I was looking through some videos I had posted on Instagram a friend had taken of me. When I watched the videos the next day, I was in awe of how good the videos turned out and how pretty I looked in them. I was shocked. I told my ex who was still my husband at the time, "Wow, these videos she took were really good. I look pretty." He replied, "But, Constance, that is how you have always looked." I looked back at him with a confused look and looked at the video again. I started to really think.

I thought about earlier that week when he and I were in Hawaii. A random teenage girl approached us when we were eating. She said, "Hi! Excuse me, I do not mean to interrupt, but I just wanted to tell you that you are so pretty. Like I really like your face." It took me off guard for sure. I said, "Wow, really...me?? (In a once again, confused manner) "Oh okay, thank you that is so sweet." Honestly, I think she was confused because I looked so confused.

So at that point, I was curious. Was that how I had always looked? I quickly went to my photo albums in my phone to see if it was true. As I started to look through my photos, it was as if I was seeing myself for the first time. Like blind folds were being taken off my eyes.

I never knew I was a "pretty" girl. I guess the more concerning part was that no one ever called me ugly, and I did not think I was ugly either. I just did not know I was pretty. I think I experienced at least three emotions all at the same time. As I stared at the phone, it was literally like an out of body experience. I cried, then sat there with my mouth wide open, then got excited, then got a little sad again. Why was this the case? How could I not know I was pretty? And why was I just now realizing it at the age of 29?

This really sealed the deal for me. I needed to go deeper. I had skeletons I did not know about and they had never been dealt with. One thing we learn as chiropractors is that you have to get to the root of the problem to correct it for good. The worst part of it all was something I had always known to be true. A person will only allow you to love them as much as they loved themselves. This revelation shook me to my core.

I was speaking with one of my cousins and she told me something that really stuck with me. She told me a story of how her church did an exercise at a women's conference. The women were asked to reflect on their childhood and their younger self. They later asked them to look at anything in their past that created trauma, at a young age, that they had never dealt with. Afterward, they had to speak to their inner child. I thought, what an amazing conference!

We, as women, are always taught to "take a licking and keep on ticking." Or in other words, "Suck it up, buttercup. Get back on that horse and ride it," for my Texas folk. Women are not allotted time to sit and deal with something that hurt them, physically, mentally, emotionally or a combination of all three. We always have to be strong, brave and keep going because of the responsibilities we have. There is just no time or safe space for us to do that.

Well, I challenge any woman or man, for that matter, to STOP! Look at yourself, like really look. You can look at the outward self in a mirror, but I am referring to the inner one. What hurt you? Who hurt you? What have you never dealt with? What have you looked past that needs your attention? I challenge you to confront those demons and skeletons! I will make you aware, this will be a painful process. It is not going to be easy for you to do. But you need to heal. Stop band-aiding those situations. The result of not dealing with them ends with trying to fill that void with unhealthy things that are causing you more hurt and more pain. That hurt and pain is then, unknowingly, given to others. It becomes an ugly cycle that continues and is passed on to the next person. Seek out therapy if you need to. Taking care of your mental health should never be anything to be frowned upon. It should actually get more praise than it does. To be aware of yourself enough to know you cannot do it alone and be willing to get the help you need shows tremendous strength and courage. No one is perfect. So why act as though we are?

Shadows are usually only seen if you look behind you. We are always told to keep moving forward and never look back. But, if we actually never looked back, how would we ever be able to tell what trail of a mess we have made along the way? Now granted, the intention is not to stay there when looking back. The intention is to correct wrongs and fix things which will create healing for not just ourselves, but also healing for those whom we have hurt in the process. Sometimes, we use that brilliant excuse of "never looking back" as a way to not open old wounds, face insecurities, face old skeletons, or just a way to avoid them altogether. However, that is usually due to a lack of self-awareness.

In life, even home life, we know sometimes you have to clean out the closet. Yes, you dread it the whole time, but you know once it is clean you will have the satisfaction of knowing it is done. Digging deeper into the dark shadows of what you have never dealt with can be scary because you are not sure if you will make your way back to the true you. But it is important to know that just because those things happened to you, they will no longer define you.

You have acknowledged them; you are no longer hiding them and so no one can make you feel insecure about them. Booyah! SELF- CONFIDENCE! But that is all you will get from me on looking into your shadow. You will have to research the rest for yourselves.

And by the way, to all my former college classmates, I would like to change my nickname from "Killa C" to "The Silent Killer." A lot of people slept on me, my abilities and what I would become, but now I move in silence and level up.

So, thank you!

What if you went through life thinking you did everything right? You die and God tells you you've done every-thing wrong?
-Constance

SHIPWRECKED

Change is inevitable. And it is the same with people. If they stay around, there's a reason and if they go, also a reason. Did it still suck to see people go out of my life? Yes, but after a while, it did not hurt or cut as deeply anymore. I could not force them to stay and it also became okay if they left. This lesson could be seen as a positive or negative. On the positive side, change will occur whether you want it to or not, so why worry about something out of your control. You may as well embrace it and go with the flow of things.

The not so pleasant lesson for me was never get too attached to anyone in my life, because right when you do, they might be gone shortly after. When this happened repeatedly, it made me want to cut off the world. I figured if no one got close to me, then they did not have the ability to ever hurt me. Before I knew it, I reverted back into a Monk of silence, back into that shell and the walls were rebuilt. All guarded by bob wire and pitched forks. No one would EVER be able to hurt me again.

I had a hard time seeing things and people for what/who they really were. I would always downplay the situation saying, "No, they wouldn't do that." Or, "Oh, I don't think they meant it like that." I always wanted to see the good in people that I was willing to overlook the things that would normally be quite obvious to most. Seeing good in people comes with its perks, but also comes with its pains. A lot of hurt came from not taking things as they were and still believing in people when they did something that seemed off putting.

Being open with you all, I believe it was because I rather not see it. If things and people were really as they seemed, then that would put me in an uncomfortable position of potentially having to let that individual go.

The pain I felt after the divorce was almost unbearable. People that were like family to me and friends all seemed to fade away, one by one and some in groups. That lonely feeling hung around for a while. I felt like there was no one I could call without judgment. No one who would understand what I was going through. No one I could call that would not try to throw me a pity party and say, "I'm so sorry," as if someone had just died. And no one who would not try to psych-evaluate me on a scale of 1-10.

I think some people were genuinely trying to help but just did not know how. Nevertheless, I felt like I had just lost everything with my decision. Sadly, even if no one else believed it, I knew it would be the right one. I also knew I would be hated and ridiculed for it for many years to come. People watched me like a hawk. Have you ever just felt like you are under a magnifying glass? Welp, I was. People watched my every move. I'm sure some wondered, is she moving too fast? Should she not take a break from working? She's a little too happy. Should she not be sad for a longer time? Everyone with *their* timelines.

I think the divorce was a shock to most. A lot of people saw my ex-husband and I as the "it couple." In reality, things had started to shift years ago. I told my mom about a potential separation the year before around Thanksgiving time. So, for me, I had already started to emotionally check out. So, when the divorce actually occurred 7-8 months later, it was not that fresh to me any longer. Of course, the actual act did have a big effect on me because it was official. It was more of a shock like, "Wow, this is actually happening." However, the emotional ties had already started to fade much earlier. It was not a decision that was made hastily and was well-thought out over and over again.

Honestly, some people were right with their assumptions on my journey. But what they did not understand was that *their* timeline for where I should be in my "overcoming divorce process" was exactly that, *theirs*. Most were unknowingly projecting their fears onto me. Again, I do acknowledge people wanted to be helpful. However, in such a delicate situation such as this, nothing really helped and most things I would just internalize. It sparked questions that made me question everything, which turned into inward insecurity. I was happy with my progress and the speed in which I was going. I did not feel it was too fast or too slow; I felt I was going according to what felt right at the time. My great-grandmother used to say, "Life does not come with a manual." After my divorce, that phrase really resonated with me. It was so true and I was living it.

It is amazing how we go through life everyday making decisions strictly based on what we felt was right. No guidance or direction. This raised several questions I had to ask myself. What if everything we thought was right in our decision making, in our relationships, with our kids, our careers, was actually wrong? What if everything we ever thought we would want out of life was actually the total opposite of everything we actually needed?

A lot of times in life and/or in business going "back to the drawing board" does not always mean a bad thing. Most of the time it just means you are given the fresh start you actually needed.

-Constance

INVISIBLE AND FOCUSED: ARE YOU PLEASED?

I was always an extraordinary person. This goes contrary to what most people believed that me leveling up was a form of revenge toward my ex-husband. No, I had ALWAYS been special. So, let's go back and introduce you to where it all started. I knew I was just a little different than most when I was just a little girl, age five.

I always watched my mom cook when I was younger. I was fascinated with how things were put together and how cooking made things so delicious. That meant anytime my mom was in the kitchen, I would push up my step-stool to the counter and watch very intentionally. Paying close attention to things and being observant has been a trait of mine since I was younger. So, one morning I thought, I am going to make my parents breakfast before they wake up and go to work. At the age of five, I had their sleep schedule down to a science. I knew exactly what I was going to make, pancakes. I had seen my mom do it so many times, I figured, "Yep, I can do that." I later realized that it became my slogan and motto for a lot of things in life.

Pancakes are easy, I thought! I had watched my mom enough to know where everything was. The pans, the utensils and all the necessary ingredients to make those pancakes. So, I waited. I am going to be honest; I do not remember if I set an alarm clock or not, but as planned, I was up before they woke up.

Quietly, I crept down the stairs, making sure not to wake anyone including my older sisters. I pulled out the pan—it was an electric skillet, pushed my step stool to the counter and began making my batter. As the pancakes started to cook, the smell of fresh pancakes was in the air. My parent's bedroom was right down the hall from the kitchen. About midway through making my stack of pancakes, I heard my mom say, "Who's up in there?" I yelled back, in the most innocent voice, "Constance." She responded, "Oh." Then, a few moments later, I heard their feet hit the floor and they darted out the room. With it being the wee hours in the morning, I think it took a second for the question and answer to register.

To their surprise (the loud gasp, give it away), there I was! On my step stool, making pancakes by myself, at five years old. Eventually, my older sisters came down the stairs due to all the commotion and they also gasped! But we all ate. I remember dad grabbing a big bottle of Pepto-Bismol and sitting it on the table. I laughed and said, "You won't need that." And I was right, they did not need it. The pancakes came out A-okay!

Five must have been my special number. Five was also the age I figured out my life's work. I remember my dad, mom and I were watching television one day. I was sitting on the floor and an infomercial came on. It was about some kids that looked so frail and malnourished. It was a Feed the Hungry campaign, but it concerned me. So, I got up and walked over to my dad. I tapped him on the knee and asked, "Daddy, what's wrong with them?" He replied, "They are sick." I was even more confused, at that point. I asked, "Why is no one helping them? I can help them." He chuckled a little and said, "You can be a doctor, then you could help them." I simply replied, "Yep, I can do that." And I did.

That became my thing throughout life. I was always doing amazing things, just most did not notice because I was always very quiet, shy and kept to myself. I never liked attention; it always (and still does) made me uncomfortable. So, a lot went unnoticed. But I knew the things I had done, even if no one saw it.

What I realized during my time of self-discovery was that although I had made significant growth in my mindset and mentality, there were still areas within my mind that I was still immature. It was hard to admit that a woman of my age had an immature mindset, but it was true. I did a lot of self-reflection and noticed I was living in a bubble when it came to reality. I still had that innocent, young mindset of unicorns and rainbows when it comes to certain things and how people really are. Learning people's true intentions triggered an abandonment issue that I had been working so hard to fix. Knowing not to get too attached to anyone because they could leave is a hard life to live.

I happened to come across a video on Instagram one day that spoke to me. It was about being a people pleaser. Prior to the video, I would have said, "There is no way I am a "people pleaser." I always saw people pleasers as weak in a way.

They would tiptoe around trying not to upset anyone and I was the total opposite of this, or so I thought. I was strong, confident and took charge when I needed to. However, as the guy in the video began talking about the traits of a people pleaser, my eyes widened–physically and mentally. Something that resonated with me was when he spoke about the person who was too nice. The one who was nice or overly nice to everyone and how that actually is a people pleaser. Not that being nice is wrong, but being nice can be a defense or protective mechanism.

"If I am nice, people won't bother me. If I am nice, people won't talk about me or at least they will feel bad when they do." Wow! Subconsciously, that was me! This was once again a direct correlation to my upbringing. Unknowingly, I was groomed into being a people pleaser. I used to say all the time, "But I am nice to everybody, so how could they not like me. I never do anything." Yep, people pleaser.

With all the chaos within my house and after seeing my two older sisters get ridiculed time after time for their actions that were "displeasing," I always told myself I would just do the opposite. (Hint: gaining the name the Golden Child) My sisters called me that, but it never clicked for me. They would say, "Oh, Constance is the Golden Child, she NEVER does anything wrong." And they were right, I didn't. I made every effort not to upset anyone, tried to make my parents proud, and earnestly sought their approval.

But ultimately the reason why I did that was because I just simply wanted my parent's attention and affection that I had never gotten. That well-rounded girl was a people pleaser and that habit had trickled into her adult life. As an adult, I found myself, even after having fallouts with my parents, still trying to please them.

It was the same thing with people in school. My sisters were always into something, whether it was a fight or an argument. The thing that kept me in the clear from their mess was people would always say, "Leave Constance alone. She doesn't mess with anyone and is nice to everybody." That certainly saved me from a lot of trouble and fights. However, I now understand that it was a form of people pleasing.

After the divorce, I became interested in a few guys, but none of them ended up working out. What made me angry was that I felt my ex-husband had played a major role in influencing those potential interests. I sat back and realized everything I knew, the people, the school, the "friends" all had some sort of ties with my ex-husband. All of our friends were mainly mutual friends or they at least knew of him quite well. This upset me to my core. How was I expected to move forward when everything I had known, since I was 18 years old, would always have the stain of my ex. Although I did not want to believe it, my whole adult life had revolved around that man. None of my friends were just my friends, my undergrad was not just my undergrad, everything had been wrapped up in him, nothing was actually mine. And when I came to this realization, I was enraged and frustrated.

Most of the "friends" of my ex-husband and I had picked a side, his.

I was the one who made the decision to divorce, so I was the one who held the smoking gun. Therefore, I was the one to blame. Although I had done my part in the marriage and in the relationship, I did just about everything a "good wife" should, but to most, that was not enough. I would say, actions speak louder than words, but I think most felt better to not look at my actions as a good wife. If they ignored the fact that I was a good wife to my ex then, they could continue to have someone to blame, which was me. Some thought my act was selfish and basically unconstitutional. But one question I had was how was that fair to the one who did their part and upheld their end?

I knew if I wanted the fresh start I needed, outside of him, I had to force a clean slate. So, I decided to disappear and become invisible for a little while. I took a few months off from any social media and did an even deeper soul search and cleanse. I know a few months for some of you might not seem like much, but for me and how active I generally was on social media, people probably thought I was dead. But it was the total opposite; it was the first time Constance was alive!

Every decision I had made for eleven years straight–what I ate at night for dinner, where I went, how long I was there, where I lived, amongst other things most in a relationship would consider before they just did it–was always made with someone else in mind. No decision I had made since I was eighteen years old in college was a Constance-driven decision. Yes, it was scary once I realized this fact because, if things went wrong, there was no one to blame. I would have to prove to myself I could make it on my own. It was painful because I knew I would have to let go of things and some people I was comfortable with. However, it was also extremely freeing.

I knew I had to create a whole new world for Constance and build from there. Yes, I was aware there was no way to erase everything about my ex-husband. But if I wanted more, then I needed to disassociate myself from anything involving him or at least I had to try.

This was a challenge! How do you scrub away almost 11 years of your life? I was not sure, but the position I was in, I had no choice. If I was ever to get the family life and kids I had always desired, career, businesses, new opportunities and more out of life, I would have to leave what I once knew, for good. And so, I did.

After months of being off the grid, honestly, I didn't know who was going to come back. I prayed constantly that God would not allow me to become cold as ice to people. I prayed that He would soften my heart that was surely turning into stone. I mean when you go through all I had been through while just being genuine to people who still misuse, mistreat, and take advantage of you, it's easy to ice everyone out. Those are the makings of how good people go bad. I did not want to be that person. I enjoyed my kindness and soft-hearted nature. But honestly, I was scared.

I was scared that woman was gone forever. Afraid that version of Constance was dead. And the fact of the matter was I did die, well the old me did. However, with a lot of cognitive behavioral therapy, life coaches, self-motivating talks, the strength given from God, the universe and His covering angels, I was able to return back to society as a new and improved version of the old me. Not only did I return to the sweet and kindhearted Constance that cared so much for others, but I returned with the strength of a small army. Also, I was ready to talk, and I had a lot to say!

I was ready to share about the revelations that occurred to me during my self- discovery and healing process. I felt it was my duty to help others get their breakthrough as well. Did that experience make me more conscious and aware of who I was letting into my space? Absolutely! But I think we all should. Protecting your space and energy is paramount. There is much more we can accomplish in a day, when we preserve our energy and not be so affected by the small, minuscule things.

The productivity level accelerates to new highs we would never imagine we could reach. I had to get out of the headspace of making decisions according to others or tiptoeing my way through life, making decisions not to upset them. I truly understood and came to the realization that it literally does not matter what you do, there will still always be someone who is unsatisfied with you. I had to just accept that, be okay with it and move on.

You cannot live your life for others. You only get one. There are no do-overs after you die. So why risk not being your true self? Not being completely happy to please people who will be dissatisfied regardless or for those we think will care but in actuality really could care less?

Whether people are happy for you or upset with you, you will still wake up the same way, put your pants on the same way, go to work the same way and do it all again tomorrow with or without the approval of others. When you build your life around trying to be what others want you to be, you will die never knowing who you truly are nor who you could have become. Most importantly, their disappointment does not stop your world or theirs from going round and round!

Live your life for you! It's a lot freer that way anyways. Just imagine all the possibilities you could have for yourself if you did not think, "yeah, but they..." at the end of what you are really wanting out of life. Imagine all the things you could do, the things you could accomplish, the places you would go, travel and explore.

Just imagine!

Rediscovering yourself isn't bad.
Hard? YES!
Painful? Sure.
Necessary? Absolutely.
But it's all in what you make it!
New Beginnings, I'm ready.
*-**Constance***

THAT KINDA
CAME OUT
WRONG

When I first started college, I had no filter. I had some much to say that had never been said. So, when I did open my month, for the first time in college, you may have guessed–IT CAME OUT WRONG. I had so much pent up anger, aggression and unhealed trauma. To see me now, how calm, cool and collected I can be is a beautiful sight. I no longer let my anger or emotions control me. I control them. After months worth of mediation, prayer, tears, therapy and discovery ,I had finally gotten to a place of peace. A place I never thought I was capable of accomplishing due to my background.

Communication in my house was non-existent. The only thing we knew to do was scream, holler or fight. So, you can imagine after 18 years of witnessing indoor Hurricane Katrina, but remaining silent through it all, it showed effects on me. Controlling my emotions is still something I am working on to this day. I tend to be very critical and hard on myself at times. The divorce process had taken such a toll on me in every way imaginable.

My "friends' ' became my enemies. People I thought would be in my corner disappeared and I was left feeling like I held the Scarlet Letter. For those unfamiliar with the Scarlet Letter, the narrative took place in a city in New England. The moral of the story was a woman who had a child out of wedlock. The city publicly shamed and humiliated the woman for all to see. The community made her wear a scarlet letter "A" for the rest of her life.

Well folks, this felt like a modern-day Scarlet Letter I was wearing. Not many wanted to be around me or support me because they felt they might also be looked down upon because of the divorce. After months of enduring such hate and spitefulness from others, I figured it would eventually go away. I was wrong. Most threw me out like trash or no longer wanted to be associated with me altogether. My latest occurrence of this was when one weekend, EIGHT months later, turned into hell week.

In October 2021, I told my ex-husband he could have all his stuff back, as in our mutual friends, colleagues, etc. I was just so sick of all the craziness that came with having mutual people who automatically kept choosing him in a situation they knew nothing about. I think what hurt me the most was the people who actually did know what happened or knew more than most about why I initiated the divorce but still chose him anyways. As I started to clear out some of the people he and I knew, there were a few I felt I had made a personal connection with that I wanted to keep. Obviously, I was wrong.

As I started to reach out to those mutual friends, I told them I thought it best I remove myself and I did not feel as though I should continue the friendship because it would once again be in connection with my ex. Some said, "No, we love you. We are not picking sides; we would love to keep you around." And so, against my better judgment, I stayed. Before I go any further, I think it is important to note if your intuition is telling you to do something, do it. No matter how painful it might be at first, it would be less painful then enduring more headache or heartache later down the line. Do not question your intuition! Essentially, it is there to assist you, not harm you.

I did this, again, with a "friend" whose energy I felt had changed toward me. Not just due to the divorce, but over time due to how successful I was becoming. That person once again told me the same, "No, I am here for you, I have always been." That was also false. However, I repeatedly ignored my intuition and decided to remain friends.

I had not posted anything publicly about my divorce because I am a very private person. I felt it was no one's business except the two people involved. People only started to realize over time by small things, such as my last name changing. Speaking of that, it is so hard when women get divorced. Men can pretty much divorce without being noticed because there are no major, visible changes that would clue someone in, except the guy not posting the woman anymore. And I am sure that even that statement would be up for much debate.

However, I am referring to women having a whole process. From name changes on everything, new social security cards, passport, social media, bills, house/property, cars, credit cards, businesses, etc. The women go through a lot over the name alone. Not diminishing the male divorcing process, but generally they do not go through as much grief as women. Also, their friends usually remain, they get overwhelming support from others and can basically move on to the next woman. But for women, it is different.

Those small things such as my last name change and no longer posting my ex made people notice I had gone through a divorce. And then it started pouring in. Everyone started inquiring what happened and if, in fact, I was divorced. However, I never came out and publicly announced anything to anyone. My ex-husband and I started the divorce process in June 2021 and it was finalized two months later in August. I kept everything about the process mainly to myself and only told a few "close" people about it. But in January 2022, almost eight months later, all hell broke out.

It was a weekend of nonstop turmoil and hate. First, that friend that I should've dropped threw shade on social media. Her post said something close to, "These newly separated and divorced folk are eager-eager to start dating again. Was the relationship really THAT bad?" Now, I had known this person since 2010 and considered her one of my best friends. We had just recently gone on a trip together in August where I felt things were slightly off, but not worth starting an argument over. Oddly enough, this was one of my personal friends, not my ex's, but she knew of him quite well. I am not sure if her post was aimed directly at me since she said no names, but for her to know I was recently divorced and wanting to get back out there after eight months, it sure as heck felt like it.

Even then, to be so insensitive to anyone who had gone through a divorce was the last straw for me. Her actions did not just offend me, but anyone in her friends list who had also experienced the same thing, if not worse, with their divorce. I did not respond to her post, but I did read the comments of many who felt the need to defend themselves. That was on Friday.

The next day, I went to dinner with a group of ladies who I initially told that I needed to take a step back from due to them being so closely intermingled with my ex-husband and his circle of friends. But one had insisted, "No, we love you. We are not picking sides; we would love to keep you around." As I got to the dinner, I could tell something was off. There were moments of awkward silence and them talking around me to each other. They started to openly talk about an event that I knew nothing about.

It was a party that one of the ladies was hosting. I was originally invited but, to my surprise, was no longer invited to due to my ex. One lady whispered while I was ordering my dinner, "She does not know about the party." I responded, "It is okay, I probably would have been uncomfortable anyway." I mean what was I to do, it was her party in the first place. So, they continued to openly talk about the event. What they were going to wear, their shoes and so on.

As you know by now, I was known to be explosive, but was trying to learn to control my emotions. They later told me a close mutual friend had gone to jail for an incident at a bowling alley and was now being held for a two-million dollars bail. That incident happened a few weeks prior, but no one cared to inform me.

I was boiling at that point and I contemplated flipping over the table.

I was about to forget ALL of my training, when something in the restaurant caught my eye. It was a sign that said, "Find your beach." I took a deep breath and sat back in my chair. I smirked and laughed a little to myself because I knew it had to be a sign from God. Anyone who knows me knows I find my greatest peace by any body of water. And so, I did just that. I remained calm which I think surprised the other ladies because they had seen me visibly explode before. I am sure they wanted to get a reaction out of me, but were sadly disappointed by my calm demeanor.

I later decided it was time to let them and a few extras go. So, I did. I cleaned house of any remaining people who had been extremely negative, jealous, unsupportive or abandoned me when I was at my lowest. I decided I would no longer hold on to people who I needed to let go of. Also, I had to let go of those who I was just keeping around to say I had people or to feel less lonely. Because nothing is lonelier than having tons of people around, but none of them really being there for you.

"I am healing. And even though it is a process, I see progress."
-Constance

A CHIROPRACTIC
STORY

It all started junior year of college at Prairie View A&M University. As a pre-med major, our biology department hosted a health conference every year. The department brought in various medical schools, medical professionals and reps to speak to us about their school. That particular year I, honestly, did not want to attend. I had a microbiology test coming up that I felt very ill- prepared for and I desperately needed to study. However, my boyfriend at the time was volunteering at the conference and asked if I could come along. I agreed to go anyhow, but did not intend to speak to any of the reps.

It was like clockwork. Right when I walked through the doors a rep started talking to me. She was the first table in the left-hand corner of our conference. I was in mid-stride walking and not interested in anything the rep was trying to say.

The representative of the school kept talking to me and invited me over to the table. I did not want to be rude so I put on a half-smile and I reluctantly shuffled over.

When I approached the table, I saw it was a chiropractic school. I instantly started back pedaling and I said to myself, "Nope, nope, nope I already know where I'm going and that's to medical school." Some of those thoughts I must have said out loud. However, it was something I had told myself since I was five years old and I had been studying for the MCAT. If I did not say my thoughts out loud, it was still as if the rep read my mind or probably my facial expression. I personally did not have anything against chiropractic, I just had never really heard or knew enough about it. I had never had a chiropractic adjustment and always thought it was just for the rich.

Nevertheless, the rep reeled me back in. We started to have a conversation about something completely off topic. The conversation was going great. By the end, I am not sure how she did it, but she had circled back to the original topic at hand. She asked if I would be interested in learning more about chiropractic and about Parker University on what was called "The Power Weekend." Still reluctant, I said, "Thank you, but I'm okay." Although it did start to sound pretty interesting, I knew the chiropractic school was in Dallas, Texas and I was at Prairie View near Houston. I had no form of transportation to get there in the first place. So, I started to gather my things to walk away. She then sweetened the deal. She said, "Wait! If you come, I will pay for your hotel and food for the entire weekend." At this point, I was sold!

"Okay, now you have my attention," I said with a small laugh. I was not quite sure how I was going to get there, but that was an offer I could not refuse. Luckily for me, one of my other biology major friends had also got invited to The Power Weekend. She agreed to let me ride down with her and her mother.

The chiropractic rep sent me an email later that week telling me to be sure to bring my transcripts. Nothing shocking there, I was going to visit a school. Why would I not need them? Oh, but there was more to it then I knew.

As I went to reply to her email, I double-checked for the correct spelling of her name. That's when I realized a small detail she had left out. She was the dean of chiropractic school.

She upheld her promise. She put all three of us—my friend, her mom and I— in the Aloft Hotel and took care of our meals for the entire weekend. Upon arrival at the school, I learned that she left out one more detail. She did not really explain what all took place at their Power Weekends.

The Power Weekend was a weekend that you spend visiting the school, checking out the class and campus. However, at Parker's Power Weekend, they also had all the attendees apply to the school at the beginning of the weekend. Then we would be told if we were accepted or not by the end of the weekend. When I heard this, my mouth literally dropped. To know the potential fate of my career could be made in less than two days was shocking to say the least.

I was there already and enjoyed everything the school had to offer thus far; therefore, I figured I might as well. So, I applied and I got accepted! I was not expecting it, but when I weighed out the pros and cons, chiropractic school was not starting to sound that bad. My pros were no MCAT!

The MCAT is a medical school entry exam required by medical schools and it was a beast. Parker Chiropractic school also offered two programs. A fast-track program which was all year round for three and half years, that would be broken into trimesters. A trimester is three semesters a year. It is equivalent to taking a fall and spring semester of college plus a summer semester. The second option was the regular program which was still all year round, but required fewer credit hours at a time than the fast-track. For fast track, our course load was almost 30 hours per Trimester equaling almost 90 hours a year. Whereas Parker's regular track program offered each trimester at about 18 hours instead of 30.

I chose the fast track program. I figured if I did not like chiropractic school, I would have only done it for a trimester. I could stop and keep preparing for medical school, so no harm, no foul. But the way it all worked out was something divine. It was literally as if God and the angels had planned the whole thing. So, I had to go for it.

What I have realized on this journey is that being a chiropractor taught me so many lessons that can be incorporated into life. When working with my patients, I always treat them specifically. I never treat one patient like the other. No BODY, whether the person or the body type is the same. I take time with my patients, analyze and figure out their specific needs. Some patients can take more pressure on an adjustment whereas others can not. I would never give the same amount of pressure or adjustment to a linebacker that I would give to a 12-year-old girl. Those are two totally different body types, body makeups and what they would each need would differ from each other as well.

I now see why it was so easy for me to get in the groove of chiropractic. It was the same thought process I used with everyone in my life. I never treated one person the same as the other because I knew their specific needs. Being an observant person helped with my analyzing process. I was the same kind, loving and fun person with all of them, but gave them all something special depending on the specific need I saw. And I think that is the key word, I "saw" people.

Either for who they were, their need and/ or their potential, when most might have missed it.

I believe this is why the connections I have with people are so strong. If you can meet the needs of someone, there is no telling how far up they can go. Most just need someone to believe in them. That is why it would break my heart if they left. I did not feel as though they had gotten all that they needed just yet and I wanted to assist in any way to make sure they reached their full potential.

However, some people you do have to release. Let them grow, find their own path and hope someone will be there for them as they do just that. Knowing this about myself always left me open and vulnerable to people trying to use me. And so that had to stop. I no longer just let everyone in and I learned how to filter through the fake love and decipher the real. Those who were genuinely there for me and those who were not.

How many doctors really just stop and take that extra time with their patients? To really try to find their patients unique needs? If they did, they would realize not only would it make them a better physician, but inadvertently also make them a better friend, sibling, partner, parent, aunt or uncle to others as well. The key is to listen. Sometimes we talk too much when at times we just need to listen.

Even when others around you do not say anything, you should know them well enough to know when something is off or wrong with them. We have to train ourselves to not only listen with our ears, but also with our eyes too.

THE INTRICATE DETAILS OF THE MIND

The prefrontal cortex, which is associated with logical thinking, can get overrun by negative thoughts, fears or consistent worry. It is essential to keep a positive mindset and think positive thoughts. As the saying goes, "You are what you eat." I have always taken that phrase literally meaning what you are feeding yourself physically and mentally. What you constantly put into your body and mind is essential.

Not everyone really believes this or some just do not take this as seriously as they should, but it is backed by science and research. The nervous system leads up to the brain, back down through the spine and then the extremities, your legs and arms. The brain is the powerhouse of the body which controls every aspect of your being and the systems that make it up.

Take the immune system, for example. In stressful situations, the cortisol levels increase suppressing the immune system. With a weakened immune system, the body is susceptible to viruses and diseases since the body's defenses are down.

Once again, all due to the example of stress. So just imagine what the body would undertake with prolonged stress?

Where does stress come from in the first place? Your thoughts. From constant thinking of something negative that is bothering you. With prolonged stress or an overrun negative thought process, the body's other systems also become affected. Dopamine, endorphin and serotonin, "the happy and calming-stability hormones" become suppressed as well.

Going back to the phrase, "You are what you eat," it is important to understand that serotonin, the calming-stability hormone and melatonin, the sleep hormone, are produced in the gut of the stomach and brain. So, this phrase still holds true. You, most certainly, are what you eat. It is important to be mindful of what you feed your stomach and your brain.

When eating and thinking badly, you might notice most that do experience some sort of depression, a short-term negative thought process or a prolonged one. That person consequently tends to have an affected appetite and trouble sleeping. This is due to those systems now being suppressed, which does not allow the body to produce those hormones as regularly or as quickly. To lose weight, fight off depression, eliminate worry, sleep better and have an over healthy outlook on life, it all starts with your thoughts within the mind.

In reality, life is 120% mental. Some people are going to get this, but for some, this message will just remain here on the page. Everything in life, how your life turns out, where you are in life and how you see yourself, all starts in your mind.

For example, someone could currently be living in poverty. But, if that person has a wealthy mindset, they will find ways out of that poverty situation. Then they will ensure and set up ways to never go back again.

For those that are mentally defined and defeated by their current situation(s), these people will remain in those situations and it will become their life.

Until people understand this concept, they will continue to be held captive and prisoners of their own minds. Limiting thought will bind them from ever achieving anything more than mediocrity or anything outside what is considered their normal. Fear can be paralyzing and again keep you captive in your own mind. The only person that can set you free is you.

A concept that we live by as chiropractors is the 3 T's—trauma, toxins and thoughts. These 3 Ts are what cause interference within your body. Interference means your body is out of alignment which inhibits your body's natural ability to do its innate functions such as the healing process. If someone could overcome these 3 things: their trauma (mentally and physically), toxins within their body (what they allow and take into their body) and their thoughts (emotional tides and behavioral response i.e. the limbic system), then they can become limitless.

LET'S TALK REAL ESTATE

C heck this out, there are two sides to business. There is personal and then there is the business. You have to check your personal at the door to make sure your business is not walking out of it. What people must realize is that outside of political views, race or social stature, if you put away the personal, there is money that can be made and personal beliefs should not affect it. Not doing a business deal with someone just because of their political views or race will keep a poor man broke. If there is mutual respect between you two then that is a greenlight to proceed.

Money knows no color nor view point and it all spends the same way.

What I have learned from my wealthy counterparts is that the only thing that speaks to someone with money is you telling them how they can make more of it.

The wealthy know a good deal when they see it.

I have come to understand there are two types of people with money. You have rich people and then you have wealthy people. Rich people have money, but they do things to show it off, buy big expensive things and tend to spend recklessly just because they have it. Wealthy people, however, have money but are interested in how to make more of it while using the least amount of their own money and time as possible. Thus, creating wealth.

The rich run the risk of going broke due to their lavish lifestyles. Do not get me wrong, wealthy people like nice things too. However, the wealthy do not wait until things become popular. Honestly, it's that technique that keeps the wealthy wealthier. They generally end up paying LESS than the average Joe for the same product. The wealthy love cutting costs, which allows them to keep more money in their pocket.

Only those foolish with money squander it, making large unnecessary purchases without having any intent of it being a vehicle to make them money in return. It is just all for show. That is a financial fool. Money is like a game of chess. You have to know where to move it and sometimes be okay making a riskier play for the greatest gain or to get to the greatest playing position on the board.

I've always heard the saying, "You have to spend money to make money" and quite frankly, that phrase used to scare me. I was so afraid of trying something like a course for a new skill and then failing or not making any money from it. Oh, the fear of losing the little money I had to begin with.

Nevertheless, after careful, thorough research and personal experience, I found that courses are the keys to unlocking the most cost efficient, fastest way to get you where you want to be or do. NOT QUICK MONEY SCAMS. Do not get me wrong. Like anything, you have good and bad so some "courses" are not good. However, if you can learn how to do something correctly the first time, it will make you the most profit quicker and give you the ability to learn from someone else's mistakes. This eliminates the aspect of you having to learn a hard financial lesson on your own. That is priceless!

I worked at a financial firm for about a year in between my decision to take a break from chiropractic. I knew I wanted my own chiropractic practice, but I did not know I would be diving into real estate soon after. At the firm, I was paid salary and commission for writing insurance policies while also learning and studying the stock market for free. Our boss was a principal on the stock market. A principal is someone who can sign off and write their mutual funds.

I had the privilege of having seasoned stock market professionals at my disposal and boy did I take advantage! I would constantly ask them questions about puts, calls, bonds, taxes and so on. Anything stock market related, I wanted to know. Sometimes our conversations would turn into hour-long stock market lessons mixed in with a little life lessons. That financial firm groomed me to be my most financially literate self I had ever been, in less than 12 months.

We always had Monday meetings where the first thing we would discuss was the stock market for about 30 to 45 minutes straight. You can imagine my first day at the office. Here I was this little Black girl with just an insurance license that had managed to work her way into a financial firm. That girl was now sitting down at a table with some of the most seasoned stock market gurus. All of them being white, older males in two- and three-piece suits. You can say I was a little intimidated, but I think I held a great poker face.

They spoke money. They never shied away, speaking openly about their financial wins and losses, sometimes down to the exact cent. Most of the time it was six-figure numbers and on occasions seven. I would sit at that table in awe, nodding my head and smiling even though I was completely lost. And although I was lost, I kept a good poker face for most of those meetings. However, there were times I was visibly and verbally impressed or excited. I knew I had finally made it to the right table. So much free knowledge. It was the type of knowledge that money cannot buy. It was priceless. I was studying and trying to pass the Stock Market's Securities Industry Exam (SIE) which would allow me to become registered and have my own dealings with the stock market. But, then COVID happened and my pay also took a hit.

I took that Securities exam three times and on my last try made a 69; you need a 70 to pass. I was furious and frustrated. My pay was predicated on me passing the exam and writing policies. I knew with my pay cut from salary and commissions to commission only, during a pandemic, was financial suicide. I knew I would be heading down a financial hole with bills, rent and everything else remaining the same which would be hard to get out of.

I had to act fast. Although I was not rich at the time, I most certainly was wealthy already in my mind. So, with the knowledge I had learned at the firm, I decided to take those remaining checks and invest into a vehicle that would make me more money in the long run. That is when I turned my 9-5 into my side hustle. During that time, I was ready and becoming a boss, but I didn't even know it. All I knew was that I was looking for something that I could afford at the time and that would generate the most money with the least amount of work. And that is when it clicked, real estate!

This was another industry I knew nothing about, but interestingly enough, I was always fascinated with real estate. Growing up, and guilty still to this day, I would drive to the most expensive neighborhoods just to see the houses and watch home improvement and interior decorating shows. I always said, "If I did not become a doctor, I would do real estate." Turns out I did both.

I had never taken a course or class on real estate previously, but I knew if I left it up to myself, I would figure it out. And so, I did. I started teaching myself the ins and outs of real estate. Learning the terminology and language so I could be present in real estate related conversations. First, I tried wholesale in real estate. I actually got a property under contract but the deal fell through. I was not familiar with anything in real estate at all but I figured I would just dive in and start trying some things within the industry. If I could just get a toe in the door of real estate, I knew I would blow the door right off that sucker.

Then I remembered my cousin had mentioned she did something in real estate outside of her job as an attorney. So, I spoke to her again about it and she said she did real estate closings on the side and it was very profitable. I thought, "Hmmmm, this could be my "in" on real estate." Therefore, I took that information and ran with it. I did hours upon hours of research and had many sleepless nights trying to figure out how to do these closings. For those who are not aware, a closing is exactly as the word says. A closing is when you purchase a home and close on it, making it yours. This is, generally, the moment you get your keys, making you a homeowner.

Then, you have a refinance closing. That is when you already own the home, but have decided you would like to lower either your monthly rate, interest rate, pull equity from your home or to reduce the years of remaining payments on the property. Of course, there are more technical terms, but this is my personal, simplified description on a refinance closing. So, when the pandemic started, I hate to say it, but it was to my benefit. The interest rates on property were so low, housing and refinance closings were in flight. I benefited from the economic downturn. This would be comparable to a "put" in the stock market.

Not only were interest rates low, I was able to fill a supply and demand need. Due to COVID restrictions, work schedule, family life and things of that nature, not everyone could get to a title company to close on their home. I decided to create a mobile real estate closing company where I would go to the clients, closing at a time and place most convenient to them. Apparently, this type of company had been around for years, but it was a privately kept secret and an easy backdoor way into the real estate industry. There was no real estate license or extra schooling involved. I did take some courses and certificates to 1.) make myself more marketable 2.) because I did not know what the heck I was doing to begin with.

Within five weeks, I had finished all my courses, certifications, background checks, became a state commissioned notary public and created my LLC. I was officially in the real estate business. And all for under $600. Yes, I was able to build and make my company off just $600. Remember, I told you I was down to just commission checks, so I did not even spend that $600 all at once. I broke up my expenses into payments. I would pay for a course or certification here and there as I received more money. Interestingly enough, I managed to do over 600 closings within my first year of business. Let's just say God had my back like chiroprac!

Let's go a little deeper into the story of real estate. I am in a real estate investing group where one of the members owns 19 homes. He had been in real estate for over a decade, but still kept his 9 to 5. Only recently, in 2021, did he finally resign from that job. That is proof that you should not judge someone else's situation. Just because someone has a 9 to 5 does not make them a bum or low class. Some people are using their 9 to 5 wisely. Using those funds to fund that vehicle that will continuously produce them even more funds.

Although, when you work a 9 to 5, working paycheck to paycheck, with no end goal in mind, what are your plans for when you are ready to retire? When living paycheck to paycheck, there are no funds left over. Do you plan to work that job, literally, the rest of your life with no retirement? The freedom real estate and being a CEO has given me is just that, FREEDOM. I can take a flight, come and go as I please, do closings when I want and rest when I do not. However, for me, my "off days" are usually me still looking up ways to either grow my business even more or looking at other potential businesses to start that will allow me to work even less, but make more money.

I am not confined to a desk or a grumpy boss that won't even let you take a one-day mental health day. Let alone a long needed two to three-day vacation without hitting you upside the head with a copy of the company policy. I wanted more. I needed more! I wanted better. To not feel like I was not living or being my free-spirited self with no restraints. I started to move by the beat of my own drum.

To most, I think it seemed I was being very irrational, reckless, out of control or going through a midlife crisis. But, once I got a taste of that freedom, I made a promise to myself I would never go back! So, I had to make it. I started pouring all of my efforts into becoming mentally ready to take on a boss role. I read books, listened to podcasts, watched YouTube, you name it. One of the most impactful books I read, which definitely made me put my game face on. was *Rich Dad, Poor Dad*. That book literally changed my life. I was ready to remember all of my training. From life lessons to college to my doctor's program to chiropractic offices to doing life insurance and finance to real estate. I had every tool I needed to bring it all home.

The things life taught me were free. But what life had taught me set me up far better than any other bought education ever could.

Always put yourself in groups, rooms and spaces that are initially "too big" for little you. It will allow you to have space to grow.

-Constance

ARE YOU A BOSS OR A WORKER?

Flashback. I remember when I was in kindergarten and we had to color a picture before we were allowed computer time. As my time approached, my teacher came to check my work. She looked down at my drawing and said, "Oh no, you colored outside the lines, Constance. I'm sorry you cannot go to the computers today." I still remember that to this day; I threw a f*n fit. Literally a tantrum, on the floor of the classroom, kicking and screaming.

Think about that. We are so programmed at such a young age to color inside the lines like robots. Following every rule and guideline without resistance. Subconsciously taught never to rebel or have our own minds, ideas or original thoughts. Even at a certain age it is customary for parents to finally tell their children that there is no Easter bunny, no Santa Claus and the tooth fairy doesn't exist. Instantly snapping their kids back in the reality that life is no fairy tale and not to imagine so much. Stay grounded.

Why is this? Why do we cut off the young imagination so early in their childhood? Because we all know it would be "foolish" thinking? And it would be foolish of them to have such an active imagination at a later age, right? Someone who can see past the norm into something more. Someone who is older and still has an imagination is considered childish, immature or just a dreamer by society. All words used to suppress and subconsciously "put a lid on" that person's thoughts, dreams, creativity and imagination. But why? Why do we feel the need or that it is our duty to keep people from thinking, dreaming and imagining things of that nature?

Is it not okay to imagine possibilities? Are we not okay with thinking about something bigger than ourselves? Why does it scare people so much that the first instinct is to shut it down? As adults, we tend to chalk it up to "master plans" and laugh it off. Discouraging the idea that something so out of the box is even possible. So much so it is a laughable concept.

A worker is someone that is okay with working their job. They are comfortable, have a nice salary and are okay with where they currently are. That is okay too. The world needs those who are willing to be workers. If not, the world would not go around and function as it does today. We need these types of minds to keep the world operating. Nothing wrong with this mindset. However, for those who are willing to color outside the lines and stand by that, you are ready.

When you get so tired, better yet, fed up with working at a job or for someone else, following their rules and guidelines to the point you start to look for a way out of the norm to make money, you're ready. You have now tapped into your Boss Brain. The real question is, who will be willing to work to get it and keep up that momentum the whole way through? Many people hate their job, but who would actually take the next steps to doing something about it or find ways to never have a boss again?

Being a boss is not for the lazy, uncommitted nor for those who play it safe. To be a boss, you have to bet on yourself, every day, be okay with going at it alone and have the confidence in your own ability to make your niche work for you.

If fear is something that controls your decision-making process, being a boss is not for you.

In this present moment is an amazing place to be in.
-Constance

PLACEMENT & POSITIONING

With all the new changes that I experienced, I feel I became somewhat of a chameleon lizard in life. I was able to show people from various positions and perspectives.

○ **Ladies**: You can be divorced and still elevate in life. You are not the scarlet letter the world tries to put upon your chest. Your dreams will still come true. You will still enjoy life just in a more free-er living life kind of way.

○ **Single ladies**: It's okay to WANT a man for love and for them to make you happy, but it is not okay to NEED him. NEED means you are incapable of loving your own self and making your own self happy. Your personal happiness cannot be given by others. When we rely too much on someone else to fulfill that need to be happy, we lose ourselves in the process. If that person leaves, you no longer have your happiness. Only you can provide that for yourself.

It is also important to not let the world, your peers, nor the "normal" woman's forced guidelines make you rush into anything you do not feel ready for or want to do. Whether it's kids, marriage or being in a relationship, the world puts so many age restrictions on a woman's life. From my personal experience, I wish I would have taken the time to discover myself first in my twenties. But to now do it in my 30s is actually incredible. The growth I have experienced in finding myself is truly one experience I will never forget. Choosing yourself is not selfish. It is love. And as I stated previously, you can only love someone as much as you love yourself.

○ **Independent ladies**: YES MA'AM!! You can stand on your own two feet! It is okay to be secure in yourself and confident about your accomplishments. Tell the world that you are not lonely just alone and you do not need a man. And if you are looking for one, the reason you have not yet found him is because you are strong, ready to grow and waiting for someone who can match!

○ **Husband or Man to be**: In this present moment, I am teaching you how to be the man or husband that I am looking for. I am showing you my love language. If you are paying attention, you would pick up on that. This is how you treat a Queen and good woman. This is how she deserves to be treated! The advantage of finding an independent woman is that she will fund herself. She wants your heart. In return, the same will be given to you, my King. How an independent woman treats herself shows you firsthand the life she desires to live. But with her ability to provide for herself, if you are not up the challenge, please make way for someone who is!

○ **Other women**: I am showing you it is okay to throw roses at other ladies' feet. Yes girl, you are still bad and this makes you no less than bad by doing this. Not everything has to be a competition. You can give another girl her props. I promise it does not take down your street credit! Acknowledging and giving other girls their high fives when due actually show your maturity and growth. Because think about it, would you have been able to do that before? No? Good! Then, that is growth, baby girl!

- **For the male friends in my life**: This taught me something about each one of you. **For those who left**, in your relationships you showed me that you abandon your women. You leave when things get tough or run when things get scary. There are weaknesses and insecurities there. We all have them. But until you admit you have them and begin to work on them, things will never change. You still need growth and you are not ready for your Queen or wife-to-be just yet. Also, free tip to any male, if your girl does not get jealous about you, she is just not that into you, my friend. If you are in a relationship with her, she has emotionally checked out.

- **Those MEN who stayed**: You showed me something as well. You play a supportive role in your relationships. You are willing to stick with your woman whether it gets tough or if things are going great. Regardless, you are willing to stick with it. You do not get scared easily and I think any girl will like that about you too.

- **Entrepreneurs:** Yes, it is possible! You can be a start up and be successful right out the gate. Put in that work, manifest, mediate, pray and keep putting that positive energy out to the universe that God created. You are about to get all that love, energy and nothing less back! Yes, when you start doing well, YOU BETTER POST IT! Because guess what? You posted about your business when you started that business, it just did not get that much love throughout the early growth phases. Now you are sharing the proceeds and benefits of that same business. However, now all the sudden, it is a flex! So, keep putting those positive vibes out there about your business! Soak up all that energy and harvest you are now reaping. It's going to come back to you!

○ **Switching Careers?** You may be considering switching careers or paths now that you have achieved your highest goal. Yes, it is okay! It can be done and done in an orderly fashion. Just breathe! Make a big enough mark in your current field. If you were to ever leave and go back, they would have missed you and welcome you back with open arms. Now that is what you call job security.

Switching over from healthcare to real estate was not as difficult as you would think. The same technical skills such as paying attention to detail and organization were required. In fact, in any profession these are always necessary skills. Do your research before jumping straight in. Take some extra courses, training and so on, to make sure your move is smooth and seamless. You have a good safety net or cushion in your previous field. You might be in a good place in your current career or extremely unhappy. But for most considering the switch, you are probably just looking to get more fulfillment. If that is you, I say yes, do it! Try it out. Remember, if you make your mark big enough when you are there, that position or one similar will always be available if you ever want to go back!

You haven't lost who you are, you're just different now and that's okay.

-Constance

SINGLE LIFE: SEXUALLY FRUSTRATED

S exually frustrated is an UNDERSTATEMENT! I actually was very shocked on this point. My ex-husband was my first and my only, so when it came to this matter that was not something I really considered going into the divorce. I went 18 years before meeting him without sex, so I figured I would be okay. My opinion changed very quickly on that, actually within only a few months after my divorce. I had a whole new perspective on "the single life" and for those who were in it. People have needs.

It is funny how society has made it out to where men think they are the more sexual beings. When in reality, God made women the ones without an off switch. Toys and other things can only get you so far. For my ex-husband and I, having sex often was never an issue in our marriage. However, sex cannot keep anyone either. There has to be more in a marriage or a relationship. So, during this single period in my life, it was really hard for me. I never had sex before him so I did not know what it would be like after him. But when it hit, it slapped!

It came to a point one night that I had to do breathing exercises. And I guess you can say I was still in a fearful mindset of thinking or just strong morals.

I wanted relations with others, but I felt if a man would be so eager and willing for me, he would have that same amount of eagerness and willingness for other women as well. I did not want to be given any type of sexually transmitted disease or unplanned pregnancy because I was having my moments of weakness. Yes, I know and am aware there are safe sex practices to protect yourself against that sort of thing, but those are not 100% bulletproof.

Some of the church folks I spoke to, after the divorce, told me my flesh was weak. However, I was married and sex is something married people do. So that still was not a concept I could really get with or understand. I had always wanted it all out of life. The husband, kids and family, the right way, with the right one. So, I guess I did have more willpower over my flesh than I thought. I was somewhat stronger than I thought, but I still had my moment. And those moments were bad. It did not help that my ex came back around several times to try to do what he and I used to.

It would have gotten the job done, but I knew that would only set him and I back, instead of moving forward. This was a tough spot to be in. I was not comfortable jumping from bed to bed because all that does is create voids of emptiness that then need to be filled with even more sex. Before you know it, your body count is more than what you can physically count.

On the other hand, although my ex-husband was someone I did know well, it would ultimately be a setback. My next concern was getting attached to someone that either did not deserve me or that I was not even seriously interested in. Last option was to just not have sex and continue to be frustrated. This was what I called being in "a bit of a pickle, no dill."

So, frustrations and all, I became celibate. Sigh, I know you are probably wondering how it is for me now? Nope, still hard! But I am finding myself having to do fewer breathing exercises, so we are going to say that is a plus.

A WOMAN'S WORLD

What I have noticed over the years is how poorly women have been treated in society. I mean, we can back-date this to centuries ago, but the fact it is still so relevant today is a shame. Women are still the most hardworking, but also the most underpaid. I do not think men realize how critical a woman is to their existence. Biblically, we can go back to Eve. Not only did she bear cramps or arguably, the one responsible for them in the first place; nevertheless, cramps she undertook. And then she bore a child.

Do men realize they would not be on this earth today if it was not for their mother who happens to be a woman? Without the nature and care that a woman gives to her baby within the womb through the umbilical cord, they would not be on this earth today. For most successful men that are with a woman, wife or girlfriend, I am 120 percent positive it was the support, love and care from a woman that allowed him to keep going when he felt weak.

Let's take Medusa for example. I really do not think men got the narrative right on who she really was. The story goes once you look at the face of Medusa, you turn to stone. But that was from a male perspective. I think what really happened was men looked upon the face of a woman, so beautiful, they could not look away and the men froze, metaphorically. The "snakes" on her head were actually dreads. Having said that, men have a very active imagination!

Did you ever stop to think God might just be a woman, hypothetically of course? Or are the male egos so big that it is something you could not possibly imagine. Eve, generally gets a bad rep. But hey, she was human. Although, when we do speak about Eve, I think it is important to know she DID start it all. If her love, care and nurturing nature were not given to the first born, for nine months, there would be no population.

Guys always like to talk about karma, karma, karma. But what if your male karma depended upon how you treat your women? Whether it be friend-ship, romance or a sibling. Is that not the definition of krama? Reaping what you sow, whatever goes around comes back around? So then why would that not work in the same fashion of how you treat a woman? As they say, in the most un-derogatory way possible, because we uplift women, not tear them down, KARMA IS A BITCH!

Recently, I have really come to understand the phrase by Big Sean more, that said, "A loaded mind is more dangerous than a loaded weapon." I have found it to be so true, because the more you know, the more you grow. As I started digging on my journey of self-discovery, I began to think outside the box. I eliminated fear from my strategies and started walking out on faith.

It terrified the people around me. To have my own mind, my thoughts, my own way of thinking was actually unheard of. Not being bound by others' opinions or by the need of validation of others, just being happy and con-tent with myself. That is something most do not do and may never actually experience. They are so bound by the rules, restrictions and expectations of others. To see someone free of all of that scared some people.

They thought, "Oh she's making risky moves, she is going to get hurt." People believed I had based my newfound success off of my past relationship which had zero bearing on my success at all. I think it was hard to conceptualize how I could elevate so quickly after my divorce. However, the truth was I always knew my ability; I was just always taught there should never be a competition between you and your partner. Women are also taught and groomed at a young age to be good, but not too much to where we overshadow our mates.

Therefore, I always just made moves from the background. I never tried to pass him. I did not want my ex to be embarrassed in a world where we are trained that men have to be the provider. And I agree the man should be able to provide, but for me, I was always longing for partnership. I wanted two individuals who both have their own, so together they can build an empire. Someone who is not intimidated by a woman who is very successful, independent and someone who would support her dreams regardless. That requires a true man.

Contrary to what most people believe, an independent woman will submit or let their guard down if she feels safe, trust him or feels if she were ever to lay down her heavy load, he would have the ability to pick it up. Which all leads back to TRUST. An independent woman does not look for his funds or wallet, she can do that herself, but by all means, she does like to be spoiled. An independent woman deserves it! However, she is more interested in how a man can add to her life rather than remove from it. Most importantly, she wants his loyalty. When building an empire, she does not want someone coming in and destroying the place she has worked so hard to build. Hint: This is why the strong, independent woman wants monogamy. She also has some shit she needs to accomplish. Independent women need a rider, affection, time and FULL attention, meaning no extra women involved. The things outside of that are just extra but these are the main things she desires.

Sadly, to most guys, that still might seem like a lot. However, if that is your mindset then you do not want a real woman anyway. Something more "microwavable" and easily accessible might be better suited for you. It is best to move on to something or someone who doesn't challenge you in that way or one that encourages you to be a better man every single day. Independent women only entertain those who they can see potential in or know are capable of rising to the occasion.

And if you were wondering if there are other little black girls and women like me, yes there are. But most will refuse to see.

-Constance

RELATIONSHIPS 2.0

Feel wholesome within yourself. Feel okay with being alone and not be lonely.

Stop trying to fill a void. Stop over attaching emotions to people so quickly without having all the facts of knowing them fully. This leads to painful sudden endings, heartbreak or heartache.

Stop depending on someone else for your own happiness. If someone leaves, it should not be devastating nor crippling. It is okay to be sad or upset, but there are levels to it. If it is devastating, you have placed way too much of your emotional dependence on them. (hint: codependency)

Stop being controlling and being able to be controlled in relationships. Stop putting yourself in a relationship position of feeling like you need to ask permission, especially when you are not even exclusively dating.

Stop adopting your partner's behaviors. That only eliminates or represses your uniqueness and individuality. Stop losing yourself because you are in a relationship. Still be an individual. Don't forget who you are, who your friends were/are, and what YOU like to do outside of your partner.

Reflection: "I often feel as though my partner retreats or withdraws when I show them emotion." Re-evaluate those relationships. Ask yourself these questions: Why do I keep picking emotionally unavailable mates? Something is attracting you to people with this behavior and them to you.

Are you attaching feelings to your mate too quickly?

Why are you subconsciously setting yourself up for a painful situation if it does not work out? "Oh, I like that my mate did this, so I love them." There are so many more layers to emotions than just the surface. Emotions should have depth, reasoning and a heart connection. True love is going to run deep. A true love will have two hearts that can speak to each other without saying a word. Even if they are miles or states apart, they can still feel the love.

We all should want to feel this emotion, but yet most of the time that level of emotion is met with fear. Fear of loving someone so deep with the possibility of ever losing them. This is the true difference between heartbreak and a heartache.

Am I overly trying to control the direction this relationship is going? We must relinquish trying to control the relationship and relinquish being able to be controlled by our partner. We have to find balance and that comes from being wholesome within ourselves.

Experience how it feels to be alone but not lonely. Some might have fear of being alone causing quick attachments or multiple partners. This can create voids when they end. Don't let your void become a black hole. Recognize your void(s) and ask yourself this question. What started that void in the first place? Do not let up until you have gotten to the root of that void and you are finally ready to face where it all started.

The question is truly "Why?" Why do I behave or act the way I do? Why am I emotionally the way I am? Why do I (or my partner) retreat when emotions are shared or involved? It generally has to do with our upbringing or past experiences. These things create a cycle or pattern of how we approach most situations. It is psychologically ingrained in us that we do this and then are left with the question of "why does this always happen?"

We must relinquish the need to *be in control* of the relationship while, on the other hand, also being careful of not *being controlled* by your partner. Once we unpack these issues such as our detachment behaviors, reappearing cycles, controls rather being controlled or the doing the controlling, being emotionally unavailable or projecting emotions too quick on our partners, then we are ready for healthy, stable, meaningful and long-lasting relationships.

Speaking personally, what I have noticed when taking a step back to get a better picture of my relationships is that I have actually been in both situations. I have been in a situation where I was being controlled but also the one doing the controlling. If you think about it, a lot of people are controlled and do not realize it because at that point, it's second nature for them. We can generally point back to our upbringing and home life growing up. Those traits follow us into our adult lives and become a generational cycle.

We see this a lot with bosses at work. A lot of the time it's a reflection of their home life. If they feel powerless and controlled by situations or their partner at home that shows at work. Work, then, becomes the only place that the boss feels they have control. In return, for a lot of bosses, having people they control becomes a vicious cycle so they project by overly-controlling others at their job. This is the "bitchy boss," the micro-manager, the boss that has a chip on their shoulder or the one that has the "H.B.I.C"- Head Bitch in Charge Mentality. However, it's not just female bosses.

A lot of men feel powerless or do not feel like the man of the house. Therefore, they find other outlets within their life to control. They have a need to control something or someone in order for them not to feel "weak" or "less of a man." However, people who do this are showing how chaotic their life really is, that they feel they have no control over most things in their life, at home or in their relationship.

It is about finding balance. For a lot of women nowadays, the word **submissive** leaves a bad taste in their mouths. This word can be more cringing for those who have been controlled in their lives. It is important to rethink this word. I know I had to. No longer am I controlled by my relationships. I do not just settle into their lifestyle or conform to everything about my partners. I am an independent thinker in my relationships. However, I have also learned to relinquish my control when necessary. I am not always right and my partner can take the reins sometimes if needed.

When both partners get rid of the "what I say goes" complex, it can turn into a healthy, enjoyable space for both of these individuals. Being submissive to each other. No one overpowering the other, both being able to admit when they are wrong and sincerely apologizing to the other. This means they will make a conscious effort not to do it again and the other accepting their apology by not weaponizing the fact their partner humbled themselves to do so. Not just one person in the relationship should make all the decisions, have all the control, nor should one person do all the apologizing.

There has to be balance. A relationship should be harmonious. That is love. Two people surrendering to each other with no one doing more than the other. Both putting in the same level of attention, affection and humility. This type of love would last a lifetime. This is synchronicity.

If you ever watched synchronized swimming, it is a perfect example of how relationships should be. Usually, the swimmers have a plan and beat counts to know when it is time for their part of the routine. One member goes up, then the next and so on. There are usually parts of the routine that include ripple effects, movements when the whole team does the same thing and moments when there is a star moment. The other teammates all pick up the one member to do a stunt move to shock the judges.

If you notice what I just said, one team member is at the top, having their moment to shine as a finishing stunt. However, it was the whole team, underwater, that no one saw that was doing the lifting. And even though that person had their moment for that performance, the next performance will likely have someone else on top, in which the team will still give that same level of support. That is the beauty of synchronicity.

That is the type of relationships we should all strive for, whether friendship or romance. Everyone playing their part, not trying to overshadow or over-power the other, an even give-take scenario.

The "Learned" List:

- I'm not willing to be in a relationship if it does not allow for me or him to have our own times to ourselves when needed.

- I do require and like attention but also need space. There has to be a balance.

- I do like someone who is genuinely sweet, kind and has a good heart.

- I do not like insecure guys. I am going to need you to be confident.

- I DO NOT like to be objectified! I am not a piece of ass nor am I a piece of meat!

- I do not like to feel like I am being controlled, manipulated nor do I like to feel obligated or focused to do anything. I am an individual with my own thoughts, beliefs and have an order in which I like to do things.

- I am happy to modify things ONLY for the right person if it does not make me dim my light, lose any of my self-awareness or my identity.

- I now can identify unhealed behavior.

- I am NOT okay with someone who does not believe in therapy and is not open to trying it. EVERY DAMN BODY NEEDS SOME DAMN THERAPY.

- I must be careful who I let in because people get attached or might try to attach themselves to me for their own needs. Leeches are stealers of my energy.

With that being said: ALWAYS PROTECT YOUR ENERGY SIS!!! Energy is powerful, use and spend it wisely.

I'm less of everything I used to be, but more of everything I've always wanted to become. I am sincerely a better me.

-Constance

HEALED

In conclusion, **heal so you do not hurt others.**

If you look at my life, family background and begin to dig, people may instantly think, "the Apple cannot fall far from the tree." And in many cases, that does hold true with people in similar situations as mine. However, there is that one percent rule that most overlook. There are those that take that fallen apple, cut the seeds out and plant a whole new tree.

For me, I am that whole new tree. I also think it is important to note that just because a "bad" apple fell off the tree does not mean the tree cannot produce healthy or good fruit.

If you have ever had a plant, you know sometimes a plant needs to be transplanted to another pot to give it a better opportunity to grow stronger, bigger, healthier and for the roots to get more breathing room.

It is the same with people.

For some, a change in scenery, placement or even more important, a changed mind, can start a brand new growing process.

"Aloha means hello but also goodbye." **-Constance**.

THE CALL & RESPONSE

They laughed, they left, they called me names, they talked about me to my face, behind my back and thought I did not know. But now, they reap what they sowed.

Who TF is Constance?

Constance is a true Queen.

Yes, her crown slips sometimes, but she has learned how to adjust it by herself and her friend's crowns too.

She is sun kissed by God with a Heavenly Glow.

She is Beautiful.

She is Strong.

She is a Powerhouse.

She is loved by her true friends.

She has the Heart of an Ox.

Her silence roars louder than a lion.

She burns brighter than a thousand moons.

She has confidence that cannot be taken.

So WHO TF IS CONSTANCE?

Constance is thee ULTIMATE woman!

KOBE.

If you know me, you know that I am a huge Kobe Bryant fan. It is interesting I had always found Kobe Bryant so fascinating even at such a young age. I followed Kobe his whole career and always felt so close to him like I knew him personally. But why? It was not until I was at a California beach on vacation that I made the direct correlation of why.

Kobe Bryant was always there for his team. Every week you could guarantee he was going to be there. Even if he was hurt, he would probably still try to play. He was consistent. You could count on him to show up, support and go out of his way to ensure his team and teammates were good. That shows so much about his character. And he was that same person with his family, not just on the court. He was the true definition of a man.

Kobe was the male figure in my life, at the time, that I could count on to show up. I knew I could watch him just about every week step up for his team. So, to me he was more like a father figure. He taught us all so much by his mentality on the court and off. How to carry and conduct ourselves. Never to quit nor give up just because things get tough. He never abandoned or jumped ship. He showed us all how to be there for our team, family and friends. Kobe taught us life lessons without saying a word. The ultimate Mamba Mentality!

So, I dedicate this section to you, Kobe "Bean" Bryant. Your presence, your embodiment of what a real man is, your skill, your heart is sorely missed still today. Thank you, Kobe, for being truly thee greatest of all time. Rest in heaven, dear soul.

Made in the USA
Middletown, DE
21 September 2022

10516386R00066